Stoicism Quotes

365 Days of Stoic Philosophy

Table of Contents

Introduction 1

365 Stoicism Quotes 2

Conclusion 124

Introduction

Thank you for choosing this book, containing 365 stoicism quotes.

In the following pages, you will find 365 stoic quotes, attributed to a wide variety of people who embody stoic principles and philosophy. This includes the ancient and original stoics, people such as Marcus Aurelius and Seneca, as well as modern day practitioners of stoicism such as Ryan Holiday and David Goggins.

You might like to read one quote each day for the next year, or simply flip to a random page whenever you are seeking some clarity, wisdom, and perspective.

Stoicism is a powerful philosophy that has been adopted and practiced by many of the greatest and most successful people. I hope that you enjoy the quotes contained within and are able to gain a new level of clarity and motivation from them. Enjoy!

365 Stoicism Quotes

1.

"Waste no more time arguing what a good man should be. Be one."

- Marcus Aurelius

2.

"We are more often frightened than hurt; and we suffer more in imagination than in reality."

- Seneca

3.

"To be even-minded is the greatest virtue."

- Heraclitus

4.

"Just keep in mind: the more we value things outside our control, the less control we have."

- Epictetus

5.

"The tranquility that comes when you stop caring what they say. Or think, or do. Only what you do."

- Marcus Aurelius

6.

"If a man knows not which port he sails, no wind is favorable."

- Seneca

7.

"How long are you going to wait before you demand the best for yourself?"

- Epictetus

8.

"I begin to speak only when I'm certain what I'll say isn't better left unsaid."

- Cato

9.

"What man actually needs is not a tensionless state but rather the striving and struggling for some goal worthy of him."

- Viktor Frankl

10.

"He has the most who is content with the least."

- Diogenes

11.

"Self-control is strength. Right thought is mastery. Calmness is power."

- James Allen

12.

"If it is not right, do not do it. If it is not true, do not say it."

- Marcus Aurelius

13.

"He who fears death will never do anything worth of a man who is alive."

- Seneca

14.

"First say to yourself what you would be; and then do what you have to do."

- Epictetus

15.

"Man conquers the world by conquering himself."

- Zeno of Citium

16.

"When someone is properly grounded in life, they shouldn't have to look outside themselves for approval."

- Epictetus

17.

"When we are no longer able to change a situation, we are challenged to change ourselves."

- Viktor Frankl

18.

"To be stoic is not to be emotionless, but to remain unaffected by your emotions."

- James Pierce

19.

"Learn to be indifferent to what makes no difference."

- Marcus Aurelius

20.

"To bear trials with a calm mind robs misfortune of its strength and burden."

- Seneca

21.

"The willing are led by fate, the reluctant dragged.

- Cleanthes

22.

"It never ceases to amaze me: we all love ourselves more than other people, but care more about their opinion than our own."

- Marcus Aurelius

23.

"How does it help… to make troubles heavier by bemoaning them?"

- Seneca

24.

"Curb your desire – don't set your heart on so many things and you will get what you need."

- Epictetus

25.

"We suffer more in imagination than in reality."

- Seneca

26.

"If you are distressed by anything external, the pain is not due to the thing itself, but to your estimate of it; and this you have the power to revoke at any moment."

- Marcus Aurelius

27.

"Warriors should suffer their pain silently."

- Erin Hunter

28.

"A stoic is someone who transforms fear into prudence, pain into transformation, mistakes into initiation, and desire into undertaking."

- Nassim Nicholas Taleb

29.

"Don't explain your philosophy. Embody it."

- Epictetus

30.

"Life is very short and anxious for those who forget the past, neglect the present, and fear the future."

- Seneca

31.

"Between stimulus and response, there is a space. In that space is our power to choose our response."

- Viktor Frankl

32.

"The mind that is anxious about future events is miserable."

- Seneca

33.

"The great law of nature is that it never stops. There is no end."

- Ryan Holiday

34.

"The robbed that smiles, steals something from the thief."

- Othello

35.

"I love to go and see all the things I am happy without."

- Seneca

36.

"Stoicism is about the domestication of emotions, not their elimination."

- Nassim Nicholas Taleb

37.

"The true hero is one who conquers his own anger and hatred."

- Dalai Lama

38.

"The things you think about determine the quality of your mind."

- Marcus Aurelius

39.

"It is not the man who has too little that is poor, but the one who hankers after more."

- Seneca

40.

"The art of being wise is the art of knowing what to overlook."

- William James

41.

"Wealth consists not in having great possessions, but in having few wants."

- Epictetus

42.

"What you're supposed to do when you don't like a thing is change it. If you can't change it, change the way you think about it. Don't complain."

- Maya Angelou

43.

"You have power over your mind – not outside events. Realize this, and you will find strength."

- Marcus Aurelius

44.

"Everything can be taken from a man but one thing: the last of the human freedoms – to choose one's attitude in any given set of circumstances, to choose one's own way."

- Viktor Frankl

45.

"I judge you unfortunate because you have never lived through misfortune. You have passed through life without an opponent – no one can ever know what you are capable of, not even you."

- Seneca

46.

"What really frightens and dismays us is not external events themselves, but the way in which we think about them. It is not things that disturb us, but our interpretation of their significance."

- Epictetus

47.

"You should live in such a way that there is nothing which you could not as easily tell your enemies as keep to yourself."

- Seneca

48.

"If what you have seems insufficient to you, then though you possess the world, you will yet be miserable."

- Seneca

49.

"Life is a shipwreck, but we must not forget to sing in the lifeboats."

- Voltaire

50.

"What we fear doing most is usually what we most need to do."

- Tim Ferriss

51.

"Misfortune nobly born is good fortune."

- Marcus Aurelius

52.

"Nothing, to my way of thinking, is a better proof of a well-ordered mind than a man's ability to stop just where he is and pass some time in his own company."

- Seneca

53.

"It is more necessary for the soul to be cured than the body; for it is better to die than to live badly."

- Epictetus

54.

"It is not daily increase but daily decrease, hack away the unessential. The closer to the source, the less wastage there is."

- Bruce Lee

55.

"The reason why we have two ears and only one mouth is so we might listen more and talk less."

- Zeno of Citium

56.

"Nothing endures but change."

- Heraclitus

57.

"Why should we pay so much attention to what the majority thinks?"

- Socrates

58.

"Order your soul. Reduce your wants."

- Augustine of Hippo

59.

"Common man's patience will bring him more happiness than common man's power."

- Amit Kalantri

60.

"No man is good by chance. Virtue is something which must be learned."

- Seneca

61.

"The universe is change, and life mere opinion."

- Democrates

62.

"No human thing is of serious importance."

- Plato

63.

"The obstacle is the way."

- Ryan Holiday

64.

"Ensure you endure."

- Maxime Lagace

65.

"Having the fewest wants, I am nearest to the Gods."

- Socrates

66.

"Move toward resistance and pain."

- Robert Greene

67.

"Problems only exist in the human mind."
- Anthony de Mello

68.

"Just that you do the right thing. The rest doesn't matter."
- Marcus Aurelius

69.

"Discomfort is a wise teacher."
- Caroline Myss

70.

"Usually, that which could have been better could have been worse."

- Mokokoma Mokhonoana

71.

"Things that were hard to bear are sweet to remember."

- Seneca

72.

"What consumes your mind controls your life."

- Buddha

73.

"Because a thing seems difficult for you, do not think it impossible."

- Marcus Aurelius

74.

"It is impossible for a man to learn what he thinks he already knows."

- Epictetus

75.

"Escaping death is a temporary victory."

- Mokokoma Mokhonoana

76.

"Be present above all else."

- Naval Ravikant

77.

"Be silent as to services you have rendered, but speak of favors you have received."

- Seneca

78.

"Do not spoil what you have by desiring what you have not; remember that what you now have was once among the things you only hoped for."

- Epicurus

79.

"Silence is often the wisest reply."

- Mokokoma Mokhonoana

80.

"A man's wealth must be determined by the relation of his desires and expenditures to his income. If he feels rich on 10 dollars, and has everything else he desires, he really is rich."

- John Davison Rockefeller

81.

"And if you want to know why all this running away cannot help you, the answer is simply this: you are running away in your own company."

- Seneca

82.

"When you arise in the morning, think of what a precious privilege it is to be alive, to breathe, to think, to enjoy, to love."

- Marcus Aurelius

83.

"The mind that is anxious about the future is miserable."

- Seneca

84.

"While we wait for life, life passes."

- Seneca

85.

"Ask yourself at every moment: is this necessary?"

- Marcus Aurelius

86.

"All vices are at odds with nature."

- Seneca

87.

"In order to protect ourselves we must live like doctors and be continually treating ourselves with reason."

- Musonius Rufus

88.

"All cruelty springs from weakness."

- Seneca

89.

"If you are ever tempted to look outside yourself for validation, you have compromised your integrity. If you need a witness, be your own."

- Epictetus

90.

"The best answer to anger is silence."

- Seneca

91.

"The best revenge is to be unlike him who performed the injury."

- Marcus Aurelius

92.

"Associate with people who are likely to improve you."

- Seneca

93.

"There is no genius without a touch of madness."

- Seneca

94.

"Live your life like you're the hero in your own movie."

- Joe Rogan

95.

"Keep your intention pure. Emotions will try to distract you. So, keep going. That's the cure."

- Maxime Legace

96.

"Every hour focus your mind attentively, on the performance of the task in hand, with dignity, human sympathy, benevolence and freedom, and leave aside all other thoughts. You will achieve this, if you perform each action as if it were your last."

- Marcus Aurelius

97.

"Give yourself fully to your endeavors. Decide to construct your character through excellent actions and determine to pay the price of a worthy goal. The trials you encounter will introduce you to your strengths."

- Epictetus

98.

"We should not, like sheep, follow the herd of creatures in front of us, making our way where others go, not where we ought to go."

- Seneca

99.

"Be kind, for everyone you meet is fighting a hard battle."

- Socrates

100.

"In anger, we should refrain from both speech and action."

- Pythagoras of Samos

101.

"He suffers more than necessary, who suffers before it is necessary."

- Seneca

102.

"Change your thoughts and you'll change your world."

- Marcus Aurelius

103.

"Many are the things that have caused terror during the night and been turned into matters of laughter with the coming of daylight."

- Seneca

104.

"Disturbance comes only from within – from our own perceptions. Everything you see will soon alter and cease to exist."

- Marcus Aurelius

105.

"Associate with people who are likely to improve you. Welcome those who you are capable of improving. The process is a mutual one: men learn as they teach."

- Seneca

106.

"In life, it doesn't matter what happens to you or where you came from. It matters what you do with what happens and what you've been given."

- Ryan Holiday

107.

"Difficulty is what wakes up the genius."

- Nicholas Nassim Taleb

108.

"What is to give light must endure burning."

- Viktor Frankl

109.

"Expect the river to be wild, surprising, and challenging. To expect the opposite is to live in delusion."

- Maxime Legace

110.

"A nation is born stoic and dies epicurean."

- Will Durant

111.

"You need not look about for the reward of a just deed; a just deed in itself offers a still greater return."

- Seneca

112.

"Your existence, my existence is infinitesimal. It's like a firefly blinking once in the night."

- Naval Ravikant

113.

"Effortless stoicism will come when you have dismantled everything in your mind that produces reactions."

- James Pierce

114.

"And you can also commit injustice by doing nothing."

- Marcus Aurelius

115.

"You can be happy if you know this secret: some things are within your power to control, and some things are not."

- Epictetus

116.

"Progress is not achieved by luck or accident, but by working on yourself daily."

- Epictetus

117.

"Everyone faces up more bravely to a thing for which he has long prepared himself, sufferings, even, being withstood if they have been trained for in advance. Those who are unprepared, on the other hand, are panic-stricken by the most insignificant happenings."

- Seneca

118.

"What upsets people is not things themselves, but their judgements about these things."

- Epictetus

119.

"Whatever happens at all happens as it should; you will find this true, if you watch narrowly."

- Marcus Aurelius

120.

"You become what you give your attention to… If you don't choose what thoughts and images you expose yourself to, someone else will."

- Epictetus

121.

"The man who lives extravagantly wants his manner of living to be on everybody's lips as long as he is alive. He thinks he is wasting his time if he is not being talked about."

- Seneca

122.

"It is in no man's power to have whatever he wants; but he has it in his power not to wish for what he hasn't got, and cheerfully make the most of the things that do come his way."

- Seneca

123.

"It is human to be angry, but childish to be controlled by anger."

- Mokokoma Mokhonoana

124.

"It does not matter what you bear, but how you bear it."

- Seneca

125.

"There is only one way to happiness, and that is to cease worrying about things which are beyond the power of our will."

- Epictetus

126.

"When a person can't find a deep sense of meaning, they distract themselves with pleasure."

- Viktor Frankl

127.

"The most effective way to understand the dissonance between our thoughts about reality and reality itself, is to consider how many times we've felt like our world is ending and how many times it actually has."

- Daniel V Chappell

128.

"If someone in the street were entrusted with your body, you would be furious. Yet you entrust your mind to anyone around who happens to insult you, and allow it to be troubled and confused. Aren't you ashamed of that?"

- Epictetus

129.

"We always have a choice as to, not what we hear, but what we listen to."

- Mokokoma Mokhonoana

130.

"Pleasures when they go beyond a certain limit, are but punishments."

- Seneca

131.

"Remind yourself that the past and future are 'indifferent' to you, and that the supreme good, and eudaimonia, can only exist within you, right now, in the present moment."

- Donald J. Robertson

132.

"Why is this so unbearable? Why can't I endure it? You'll be embarrassed to answer."

- Marcus Aurelius

133.

"We're never unhappy until we remember why we're supposed to be unhappy."

- Daniel V Chappell

134.

"If you anticipate the coming of troubles, you take away their power when they arrive."

- Seneca

135.

"There is a limit to the time assigned you, and if you don't use it to free yourself it will be gone and never return."

- Marcus Aurelius

136.

"Only time can heal what reason cannot."

- Seneca

137.

"Nothing ever goes away until it teaches us what we need to know."

- Pema Chodron

138.

"Death smiles at us all. All a man can do is smile back."

- Marcus Aurelius

139.

"Everything that happens is either endurable or not. If it's endurable, then endure it. Stop complaining. If it's unendurable... then stop complaining. Your destruction will mean its end as well. Just remember: you can endure anything your mind can make endurable, by treating it as in your interest to do so."

- Marcus Aurelius

140.

"Much of what other people know isn't worth knowing."

- Nicholas Taleb

141.

"Uncertainty is an uncomfortable position. But certainty is an absurd one."

- Voltaire

142.

"A man is no bigger than the smallest thing that provokes him."

- Dan Horton

143.

"True rewards – wealth, knowledge, love, fitness, and equanimity – come from ignoring others and improving ourselves."

- Naval Ravikant

144.

"Learn to detach yourself from the chaos of the battlefield."

- Robert Greene

145.

"A fool is a man who disregards legacy."

- Daniel V Chappell

146.

"A man is as unhappy as he has convinced himself he is."

- Seneca

147.

"What are virtues, if not practiced evenly in both times of joy and in hardships."

- Tiisetso Maloma

148.

"Tomorrow's worries contaminate the present."

- Tiisetso Maloma

149.

"Reject your sense of injury, and the injury itself disappears."

- Marcus Aurelius

150.

"The impediment to action advances action. What stands in the way becomes the way."

- Marcus Aurelius

151.

"Any person capable of angering you becomes your master."

- Epictetus

152.

"Sometimes even to live is an act of courage."

- Seneca

153.

"You're better off not giving the small things more time than they deserve."

- Marcus Aurelius

154.

"I cannot teach anybody anything, I can only make them think."

- Socrates

155.

"Don't allow yourself to be heard any longer griping about public life, not even with your own ears."

- Marcus Aurelius

156.

"Disgraceful if, in this life where your body does not fail, your soul should fail you first."

- Marcus Aurelius

157.

"Where you arrive does not matter as much as what sort of person you are when you arrive there."

- Seneca

158.

"Men seek out retreats for themselves in the country, by the seaside, on the mountains… nowhere can a man find a retreat more peaceful or more free from trouble than his own soul."

- Marcus Aurelius

159.

"Understand what you can control and what you can't. Forget about the things you can't control and put that energy into the things you can control."

- Shane Parrish

160.

"Intelligence consists in ignoring things that are irrelevant."

- Nassim Nicholas Taleb

161.

"The wise man listens to meaning, the fool only gets the noise."

- Nassim Nicholas Taleb

162.

"You can change it, you can accept it, or you can leave it. What is not a good option is to sit around wishing you would change it but not changing it, wishing you would leave it but not leaving it, and not accepting it."

- Naval Ravikant

163.

"True happiness is to enjoy the present, without anxious dependence upon the future, not to amuse ourselves with either hopes or fears but to rest satisfied with what we have, which is sufficient, for he that is so wants nothing."

- Seneca

164.

"Until we have begun to go without them, we fail to realize how unnecessary many things are. We've been using them not because we needed them but because we had them."

- Seneca

165.

"Our life is what our thoughts make it."

- Marcus Aurelius

166.

"Luck is what happens when preparation meets opportunity."

- Seneca

167.

"Everything we hear is an opinion, not a fact. Everything we see is a perspective, not the truth."

- Marcus Aurelius

168.

"The difference between stupidity and genius is that genius has its limits."

- Albert Einstein

169.

"He who is not a good servant will not be a good master."

- Plato

170.

"Thinking is difficult, that's why most people judge."

- Carl Jung

171.

"We are what we repeatedly do. Excellence is not an act, but a habit."

- Aristotle

172.

"The man who asks a question is a fool for a minute. The man who does not ask, is a fool for life."

- Confucius

173.

"Other people's mistakes? Leave them to their makers."

- Marcus Aurelius

174.

"We are disturbed not by things, but by the view which we take of them."

- Epictetus

175.

"Treat your inferiors in the way in which you would like to be treated by your own superiors."

- Seneca

176.

"Rejection of desire is liberating. Renunciation is a form of power."

- Kilroy J. Oldster

177.

"Pitying a living man for being poor is like envying a dead man for being rich."

- Mokokoma Mokhonoana

178.

"It is a rare blessing to see accept things, and people, as they are."

- Mokokoma Mokhonoana

179.

"All that exists is the seed of what will emerge from it."

- Marcus Aurelius

180.

"In your actions, don't procrastinate. In your conversations, don't confuse. In your thoughts, don't wander. In your soul, don't be passive or aggressive. In your life, don't be all about business."

- Marcus Aurelius

181.

"Expectation is the only seed of disappointment."

- Mokokoma Mokhonoana

182.

"The first principle of practical stoicism is this: we don't react to events; we react to our judgements about them, and the judgements are up to us."

- Ward Farnsworth

183.

"Making noble resolutions is not as important as keeping the resolutions you have made already."

- Seneca

184.

"Sometimes, even to live is an act of courage."

- Seneca

185.

"The willing are led by fate, the reluctant are dragged."

- Cleanthes of Assos

186.

"Being a Stoic does not mean being a robot. Being a Stoic means remaining calm both at the height of pleasure and the depths of misery."

- Abhijit Naskar

187.

"We might never rid ourselves of a lingering anxiety regarding our death; this is a kind of tax we pay in return for self-awareness."

- Derren Brown

188.

"Life is how you look at it."

- Mokokoma Mokhonoana

189.

"That which Fortune has not given, she cannot take away."

- Seneca

190.

"Take a deep breath. Get present in the moment and ask yourself what is important this very second."

- Greg McKeown

191.

"The world might call you a pessimist. Who cares? It's far better to seem like a downer than to be blindsided or caught off guard."

- Ryan Holiday

192.

"You cannot overestimate the unimportance of practically everything."

- Greg McKeown

193.

"No man is free who is not master of himself."

- Epictetus

194.

"If change is forced upon you, you must resist the temptation to overreact or feel sorry for yourself."

- Robert Greene

195.

"Self-discipline and self-control determine the quality of your life more than anything else."

- Ed Latimore

196.

"He who angers you conquers you."

- Elizabeth Kenny

197.

"He who reigns within himself, and rules passions, desires, and fears, is more than a king."

- John Milton

198.

"Self-control is the chief element in self-respect, and self-respect is the chief element in courage."

- Thucydides

199.

"If you lose self-control, everything will fall."

- John Wooden

200.

"Be true to whoever or whatever you are and wear it like a badge of honor. Fit in with one person and one person only: yourself."

- David Goggins

201.

"There is no better way to grow as a person than to do something you hate every day."

- David Goggins

202.

"You find peace by coming to terms with what you don't know."

- Nassim Nicholas Taleb

203.

"What matters most is not what our obstacles are but how we see them, how we react to them, and whether we keep our composure."

- Ryan Holiday

204.

"Stop trying to impress others with your stuff and start trying to impress them with your life."

- Joshua Becker

205.

"The Sage desires only one thing, virtue, and he is cautious about only one thing, vice. He is the same in every circumstance because what is most important lies within him, and not with external events, which are constantly changing."

- Donald J. Robertson

206.

"You should, I need hardly say, live in such a way that there is nothing which you could not as easily tell your enemy as keep to yourself."

- Seneca

207.

"Show me a man who though sick is happy, who though in danger is happy, who though in prison is happy, and I'll show you a Stoic."

- Epictetus

208.

"You will continue to suffer if you have an emotional reaction to everything that is said to you. True power is sitting back and observing everything with logic. If words control you, that means everyone else can control you. Breathe, and allow things to pass."

- Bruce Lee

209.

"Life is really simple, but we insist on making it complicated."

- Confucius

210.

"To avoid criticism: say nothing, do nothing, be nothing."

- Aristotle

211.

"No one is more hated than he who speaks the truth."

- Plato

212.

"You can't change how people treat you or what they say about you. All you can do is change how you react to it."

- Mahatma Gandhi

213.

"All cruelty springs from weakness."

- Seneca

214.

"If a little is not enough for you, then nothing is."

- Epicurus

215.

"Be tolerant with others and strict with yourself."

- Marcus Aurelius

216.

"When the debate is lost, slander becomes the tool of the losers."

- Socrates

217.

"True affluence is not needing anything."

- Gary Snyder

218.

"Progress daily in your own uncertainty. Live in awareness of the questions."

- Bremer Acosta

219.

"Seek not for events to happen as you wish, but rather wish for events to happen as they do, and your life will go smoothly."

- Epictetus

220.

"All outdoors may be bedlam, provided there is no disturbance within."

- Seneca

221.

"The greatest obstacle to living is expectancy, which hangs upon tomorrow and loses today. You are arranging what is in Fortune's control and abandoning what lies in yours."

- Seneca

222.

"When force of circumstance upsets your equanimity, lose no time in recovering your self-control, and do not remain out of tune longer than you can help. Habitual recurrence to the harmony will increase your mastery of it."

- Marcus Aurelius

223.

"Together with intelligence, self-control turns out to be the best predictor of a successful and satisfying life."

- Steven Pinker

224.

"Growth and comfort do not coexist."

- Ginny Rometty

225.

"The key to growth is the introduction of higher dimensions of consciousness into our awareness."

- Lao Tzu

226.

"We must remember: there is no easy way."

- Ryan Holiday

227.

"True Stoics don't care about the outcome. They just care to give their best shot, right here, right now."

- Maxime Legace

228.

"Genius often really is just persistence in disguise."

- Ryan Holiday

229.

"The more time you spend in your discomfort zone, the more your comfort zone will expand."

- Robin Sharma

230.

"Raise your words, not your voice. It is the rain that grows flowers, not thunder."

- Rumi

231.

"Get busy with life's purpose, toss aside empty hopes, get active in your own rescue."

- Marcus Aurelius

232.

"When you arise in the morning, think what a precious privilege it is to be alive, to breathe, to think, to enjoy, to love."

- Marcus Aurelius

233.

"Prejudices are what fools use for reason."

- Francois Voltaire

234.

"The most dangerous person is the one who listens, thinks, and observes."

- Bruce Lee

235.

"Cultivate a fearless approach to life, attack everything with boldness and energy."

- Robert Greene

236.

"True success is achieved by stretching oneself, learning to feel comfortable being uncomfortable."

- Ken Poirot

237.

"It takes courage to accept life fully, to say yes to our life, yes to our karma, yes to our mind, emotions, and whatever else unfolds."

- Dzigar Kongtrul Rinpoche

238.

"I like to see what I'm made of. I want to see if there's a limit to the human soul."

- David Goggins

239.

"Comfort makes you weaker. We need some variability, some stressors. Not too much, but just enough."

- Nassim Nicholas Taleb

240.

"The path to success will leave you callused, bruised, and very tired. It will also leave you empowered."

- David Goggins

241.

"True will is quiet humility, resilience, and flexibility; the other kind of will is weakness disguised by bluster and ambition."

- Ryan Holiday

242.

"This is the mark of perfection of character – to spend each day as if it were your last, without frenzy, laziness, or any pretending."

- Marcus Aurelius

243.

"In the meantime, cling tooth and nail to the following rule: not to give in to adversity, not to trust prosperity, and always take full note of Fortune's habit of behaving just as she pleases."

- Seneca

244.

"Let us not postpone anything, let us engage in combats with life each day."

- Seneca

245.

"Even the least of our activities ought to have some end in view."

- Marcus Aurelius

246.

"Regard a friend as loyal, and you will make him loyal."

- Seneca

247.

"What fortune has made yours is not your own."

- Seneca

248.

"Sometimes in life we must fight not only without fear, but also without hope."

- Alessandro Pertini

249.

"Never discourage anyone who continually makes progress – no matter how slow."

- Plato

250.

"Stop thinking, and end your problems."

- Lao Tzu

251.

"No man has the right to be an amateur in the matter of physical training. It is a shame for a man to grow old without seeing the beauty and strength of which his body is capable."

- Socrates

252.

"Learn to be indifferent to what makes no difference."

- Marcus Aurelius

253.

"Remember this: very little is needed to make a happy life."

- Marcus Aurelius

254.

"A seed grows with no sound, but a tree falls with huge noise. Destruction has noise, but creation is quiet. This is the power of silence… Grow silently."

- Confucius

255.

"The important thing about a problem is not its solution, but the strength we gain in finding the solution."

- Seneca

256.

"Never interrupt your enemy when he is making a mistake."

- Sun Tzu

257.

"Who looks outside, dreams; who looks inside, awakes."

- Carl Jung

258.

"The moment you accept yourself, you grow."

- Xan Oku

259.

"I know you won't believe me, but the highest form of human excellence is to question oneself and others."

- Socrates

260.

"When a person can't find a deep sense of meaning, they distract themselves with pleasure."

- Viktor Frankl

261.

"There are two ways to get enough. One is to accumulate more and more. The other is to desire less."

- G.K. Chesterton

262.

"Be happy for this moment. This moment is your life."

- Marcus Aurelius

263.

"Knowledge speaks, but wisdom listens."

- Jimi Hendrix

264.

"While we wait for life, life passes."

- Seneca

265.

"We cannot have it both ways: if we are free, we are responsible: if we are not responsible, we are not free."

- Fulton Sheen

266.

"The aim of argument, or discussion, should not be victory, but progress."

- Joseph Joubert

267.

"It's not that we have little time, but more that we waste a good deal of it."

- Seneca

268.

"Begin at once to live, and count each separate day as a separate life."

- Seneca

269.

"Concentrate every minute like a Roman – like a man – on doing what's in front of you with precise and genuine seriousness, tenderly, willingly, with justice. And on freeing yourself from all other distractions."

- Marcus Aurelius

270.

"The ordinary objects of human endeavor, property, outward success, luxury – have always seemed to me contemptible."

- Albert Einstein

271.

"The meaning of life is just to be alive. It is so plain and so obvious and so simple. And yet, everybody rushes around in a great panic as if it were necessary to achieve something beyond themselves."

- Alan Watts

272.

"When we become fixed in our perceptions, we lose our ability to fly."

- Mingyur Rinpoche

273.

"Remember that your perception of the world is a reflection of your state of consciousness."

- Eckhart Tolle

274.

"Understand: in life as in war, nothing ever happens just as you expect it to."

- Robert Greene

275.

"Be disentangled from all perceptions. They are not you."

- Brian Thompson

276.

"Realists are not afraid to look at the harsh circumstances of life."

- Robert Greene

277.

"Assume life will be really tough, and then ask if you can handle it. If the answer is yes, you've won."

- Charlie Munger

278.

"The fundamental delusion – there is something out there that will make me happy and fulfilled forever."

- Naval Ravikant

279.

"Most of what we say and do is not essential. If you can eliminate it, you'll have more time, and more tranquility. Ask yourself at every moment: is this necessary?"

- Marcus Aurelius

280.

"If you seek tranquility, do less. Or (more accurately) do what's essential – what the reason of a social being requires, and in the requisite way. Which brings a double satisfaction: to do less, better."

- Marcus Aurelius

281.

"Anger, if not restrained, is frequently more hurtful to us than the injury that provokes it."

- Seneca

282.

"The good and the wise lead quiet lives."

- Euripides

283.

"It's not what we have in life, but who we have in our life that matters."

- J.M. Lawrence

284.

"The real man smiles in trouble, gathers strength from distress, and grows brave by reflection."

- Thomas Paine

285.

"To know what people really think, observe what they do, not what they say."

- Descartes

286.

"Everything hangs on ones thinking… A man is as unhappy as he has convinced himself he is."

- Seneca

287.

"The happiness of those who want to be popular depends on others; the happiness of those who seek pleasure fluctuates with moods outside their control; but the happiness of the wise grows out of their own free acts."

- Marcus Aurelius

288.

"All you need are these: certainty of judgment in the present moment; action for the common good in the present moment; and an attitude of gratitude in the present moment for anything that comes your way."

- Marcus Aurelius

289.

"I am happy because I want nothing from anyone. I do not care for money. Decorations, titles, or distinctions mean nothing to me. I do not crave praise. The only thing that gives me pleasure, apart from my work, my violin, and my sailboat, is the appreciation of my fellow workers."

- Albert Einstein

290.

"When you transform your mind, everything you experience is transformed."

- Mingyur Rinpoche

291.

"We humans are unhappy in large part because we are insatiable; after working hard to get what we want, we routinely lose interest in the object of our desire. Rather than feeling satisfied, we feel a bit bored, and in response to this boredom, we go on to form new, even grander desires."

- William B. Irvine

292.

"The most important reason to live in the moment is that nothing lasts forever. Enjoy the moment while it's in front of you. Be present. Accept life for what it is: a finite span of time with infinite possibilities."

- Joshua Fields Millburn

293.

"Happiness is not to acquire and enjoy, but nothing to be desired, as it is to be free."

- Epictetus

294.

"It is impossible that happiness, and yearning for what is not present, should ever be united."

- Epictetus

295.

"There is only one way to happiness, and that is to cease worrying about things which are beyond the power of our will."

- Epictetus

296.

"Happiness is a choice that requires effort at times."

- Aeschylus

297.

"The goal of life is living in agreement with nature."

- Zeno of Citium

298.

"As long as you remember that everything is exactly how it's supposed to be, you will always be sane."

- Alan Watts

299.

"Don't demand or expect that events happen as you would wish them to. Accept events as they actually happen. That way, peace is possible."

- Epictetus

300.

"Once you've truly controlled your own fate, for better or for worse, you'll never let anyone else tell you what to do."

- Naval Ravikant

301.

"Human beings want control and certainty. 'Accepting fate' means the opposite. That's why it seems absurd to us."

- Maxime Lagace

302.

"Everything comes and goes in life. Happiness and unhappiness are temporary experiences that rise from sense perception. Heat and cold, pleasure and pain, will come and go. They never last forever. So, do not get attached to them. We have no control over them."

- Krishna

303.

"In all things, we should try to make ourselves be as grateful as possible."

- Seneca

304.

"Everywhere, at each moment, you have the option: to accept this event with humility; to treat this person as he should be treated; to approach this thought with care, so that nothing irrational creeps in."

- Marcus Aurelius

305.

"Focus on what nature demands, as if you were governed by that alone. Then do that, and accept it, unless your nature as a living being would be degraded by it."

- Marcus Aurelius

306.

"Whatever happens to you has been waiting to happen since the beginning of time."

- Marcus Aurelius

307.

"Each of us needs what nature gives us, when nature gives it."

- Marcus Aurelius

308.

"Man's character is his fate."

- Heraclitus

309.

"He who does not desire or fear the uncertain day or capricious fate, is equal to the gods above and loftier than mortals."

- Justus Lipsius

310.

"First, see clearly. Next, act correctly. Finally, endure and accept the world as it is."

- Ryan Holiday

311.

"Accept things to which fate binds you, and love the people with whom fate brings you together, but do so with all your heart."

- Marcus Aurelius

312.

"Don't let your fears paralyze you into becoming a lesser version of yourself. Eliminate fear by confronting what you're afraid of."

- David Goggins

313.

"We define ourselves far too often by our past failures. That's not you. You are this person right now. You're the person who has learned from those failures."

- Joe Rogan

314.

"Many of the anxieties that harass you are superfluous... expand into an ampler region, letting your thoughts sweep over the entire universe."

- Marcus Aurelius

315.

"Repeated failure will toughen your spirit and show you with absolute clarity how things must be done."

- Robert Greene

316.

"Fear is a natural reaction to moving closer to the truth."

- Pema Chodron

317.

"No amount of anxiety makes any difference to anything that is going to happen."

- Alan Watts

318.

"Withstand the setbacks and failures, the days of drudgery, and the hard work that are always a part of any creative action."

- Robert Greene

319.

"Life's three best teachers: heartbreak, empty pockets, failures."

- Haemin Sunim

320.

"Don't let fear, low self-esteem, and the negative voices hold you back from your true destiny."

- David Goggins

321.

"Learn to fail with pride – and do so fast and cleanly. Maximize trial and error – by mastering the error part."

- Nassim Nicholas Taleb

322.

"If you are ever tempted to look for outside approval, realize that you have compromised your integrity. If you need a witness, be your own."

- Epictetus

323.

"Focus on the moment, not on the monsters that may or may not be up ahead."

- Ryan Holiday

324.

"Don't grieve. Anything you lose comes around in another form."

- Rumi

325.

"Death smiles at us all, but all a man can do is smile back."

- Marcus Aurelius

326.

"You could leave life right now. Let that determine what you do and say and think."

- Marcus Aurelius

327.

"Life has more meaning in the face of death."

- Robert Greene

328.

"Things you won't say on your deathbed: I wish I paid more attention to what other people think."

- Johnny Uzan

329.

"By becoming deeply aware of our mortality, we intensify our experience of every aspect of life."

- Robert Greene

330.

"Life is all the more precious and beautiful because it is so fleeting."

- Jack Kornfield

331.

"I'm not afraid of dying. I'm afraid not to have lived."

- Wim Hof

332.

"There is no cure for birth and death save to enjoy the interval."

- George Santayana

333.

"By contemplating the impermanence of everything in the world, we are forced to recognize that every time we do something could be the last time we do it, and this recognition can invest the things we do with a significance and intensity that would otherwise be absent."

- William B. Irvine

334.

"Since every man dies, it is better to die with distinction than to live long."

- Musonius Rufus

335.

"It is better to conquer grief than to deceive it."

- Seneca

336.

"Let us prepare our minds as if we'd come to the very end of life. Let us postpone nothing."

- Seneca

337.

"The best answer to anger is silence."

- Marcus Aurelius

338.

"It is our own opinions that disturb us. Take away these opinions then, and resolve to dismiss your judgment about an act as if it were something grievous, and your anger is gone."

- Marcus Aurelius

339.

"Being angry means your lizard brain took control. Being calm means you stayed above your emotions."

- Maxime Legace

340.

"Yes, you can – if you do everything as if it were the last thing you were doing in life, and stop being aimless, stop letting your emotions override what your mind tells you, stop being hypocritical, self-centered, irritable."

- Marcus Aurelius

341.

"At any given moment, you can choose to follow the chain of thoughts, emotions, and sensations that reinforce a perception of yourself as vulnerable and limited, or to remember that your true nature is pure, unconditioned, and incapable of being harmed."

- Mingyur Rinpoche

342.

"Your true self is not your emotion such as anger, frustration, or hate. It is the inner witness that knows the rise and fall of your emotion."

- Haemin Sunim

343.

"Greatness starts with the replacement of hatred with polite disdain."

- Nassim Nicholas Taleb

344.

"If we seek social status, we give other people power over us: we have to do things calculated to make them admire us, and we have to refrain from doing things that will trigger their disfavor."

- William B. Irvine

345.

"Zoom out. In the grand scheme of things, is this really going to affect you? We can't even remember what we were doing 5 days ago, let alone 5 years. What matters is how you feel now. If it makes you upset, let it go. If it feels good, let it consume you."

- Thibaut

346.

"Once the ego inflates, it will only come back to earth through some jarring failure."

- Robert Greene

347.

"Do not envy those who seem naturally gifted; it is often a curse."

- Robert Greene

348.

"When you think you're done, you're only at 40% of your body's capability."

- David Goggins

349.

"You're never given more pain than you can handle."

- Byron Katie

350.

"Even if you are hurting, never let your competition see the look of defeat or even vulnerability on your face."

- David Goggins

351.

"What is the point of dragging up sufferings that are over, of being miserable now, because you were miserable then?

- Seneca

352.

"You don't suffer because things are impermanent. You suffer because things are impermanent, and you think they are permanent."

- Thich Nhat Hanh

353.

"Pain is neither intolerable nor everlasting if you bear in mind that it has its limits, and if you add nothing to it in imagination."

- Marcus Aurelius

354.

"The pain and boredom we experience in the initial stage of learning a skill toughens our minds."

- Robert Greene

355.

"We must be willing to roll the dice and lose. Prepare, at the end of the day, for none of it to work."

- Ryan Holiday

356.

"All greatness comes from suffering."

- Naval Ravikant

357.

"The path of least resistance is a terrible teacher."

- Ryan Holiday

358.

"Pay attention to your enemies, for they are the first to discover your mistakes."

- Antisthenes

359.

"Accustom yourself to criticism."

- Robert Greene

360.

"We find comfort among those who agree with us – growth among those who don't."

- Frank A. Clark

361.

"Your reputation is harmed the most by what you say to defend it."

- Nassim Nicholas Taleb

362.

"If evil be spoken of you and it be true, correct yourself, if it's a lie, laugh at it."

- Epictetus

363.

"Love without sacrifice is theft."

- Nassim Nicholas Taleb

364.

"If you want to improve, be content to be thought foolish and stupid."

- Epictetus

365.

"Lean into the discomfort of the work."

- Brene Brown

Conclusion

Thanks again for choosing this book.

I hope you have enjoyed the stoicism quotes contained within, and that they have been able to provide you with clarity, motivation, and perspective.

If you enjoyed this book, please do not hesitate to share it with a friend and pass on the wisdom and power that stoicism can provide!

www.ingramcontent.com/pod-product-compliance
Lightning Source LLC
LaVergne TN
LVHW011721060526
838200LV00051B/2981